Brighter Days of Hope

A 31-Day Devotional

Brighter Days of Hope

of

Hope

A 31-Day Devotional

Lisa Cassman

Halo
PUBLISHING
INTERNATIONAL

No part of this publication may be reproduced, stored in a retrieval system or transmitted in any form or by any means, electronic, mechanical, photocopying, recording or otherwise, without prior permission of Halo Publishing International.

The views and opinions expressed in this book are those of the author and do not necessarily reflect the official policy or position of Halo Publishing International. Any content provided by our authors are of their opinion and are not intended to malign any religion, ethnic group, club, organization, company, individual or anyone or anything.

No generative artificial intelligence (AI) was used in the writing of this work. The author expressly prohibits any entity from using this publication to train AI technologies to generate text, including, without limitation, technologies capable of generating works in the same style or genre as this publication.

For permission requests, write to the publisher, addressed "Attention: Permissions Coordinator," at the address below.

Hal**o**
PUBLISHING
INTERNATIONAL

Halo Publishing International
7550 W IH-10 #800, PMB 2069,
San Antonio, TX 78229

First Edition, August 2025
ISBN: 978-1-63765-807-9
Library of Congress Control Number: 2025914511

The information contained within this book is strictly for informational purposes. Unless otherwise indicated, all the names, characters, businesses, places, events and incidents in this book are either the product of the author's imagination or used in a fictitious manner. Any resemblance to actual persons, living or dead, or actual events is purely coincidental.

Halo Publishing International is a self-publishing company that publishes adult fiction and non-fiction, children's literature, self-help, spiritual, and faith-based books. We continually strive to help authors reach their publishing goals and provide many different services that help them do so. We do not publish books that are deemed to be politically, religiously, or socially disrespectful, or books that are sexually provocative, including erotica. Halo reserves the right to refuse publication of any manuscript if it is deemed not to be in line with our principles. Do you have a book idea you would like us to consider publishing? Please visit www.halopublishing.com for more information.

I dedicate this book, with the hope that comes through the Lord, to the memory of my aunt Tina. She shared her hope daily; her faith never wavered, and she was never ashamed to let others know where she stood with the Lord. She was a prayer warrior who never doubted what God could do for us.

Thank you, Ernie, for reminding us daily how the Lord has gotten you through these tough times. Rejoicing for her as she went home to the Lord, even as your heart hurts as you miss her.

For each person who reads this devotional, I pray that you can come to know and trust the Lord and find the joy and hope you so deserve. Brighter days are ahead.

Contents

Whoever dwells in the shelter of the Most High
will rest in the shadow of the Almighty
I will say of the Lord, "He is my refuge
and my fortress,
my God, in whom I trust."

Surely He will save you
from the fowler's snare
and from the deadly pestilence.
He will cover you with His feathers,
and under His wings you will find refuge;
His faithfulness will be your shield and rampart.
You will not fear the terror of night,
nor the arrow that flies by day,
nor the pestilence that stalks in the darkness,
nor the plague that destroys at midday.
A thousand may fall at your side,
ten thousand at your right hand,
but it will not come near you.
You will only observe with your eyes
and see the punishment of the wicked.

If you say, "The Lord is my refuge,"
and you make the Most High your dwelling,
no harm will overtake you,
no disaster will come near your tent.
For He will command his angels concerning you
to guard you in all your ways;
they will lift you up in their hands,
so that you will not strike your foot against a stone.
You will tread on the lion and the cobra;
you will trample the great lion and the serpent.

"Because he loves Me," says the Lord,
"I will rescue him;
I will protect him, for he acknowledges My name.
He will call on Me, and I will answer him;
I will be with him in trouble,
I will deliver him and honor him.
With long life I will satisfy him
and show him my salvation."

(Psalm 91, New International Version)

Day 1

May the God of hope fill you with
all joy and peace as you trust in Him,
so that you may overflow with hope
by the power of the Holy Spirit.

(Romans 15:13)

Do you trust God enough to know that He fills you with hope? He has promised us that, no matter what has happened in our life, He has our back, and He will be there for us. Our life is filled with good and bad, but God is with us, no matter what has happened or what is about to happen. Are you able to see the hope through your eyes that may have been deceived by something that has gotten you down?

Take a moment to write the joys you feel because of the hope He has given you.

What gives you peace and understanding that can fill you with God's hope?

Prayer:

Lord, help me to see and feel Your hope in all circumstances, not just through the brighter days and nights. I want to keep Your joy and peace going and feel it with everyday hope.

Day 2

"For I know the plans I have for you,"
declares the Lord, "plans to prosper you
and not to harm you, plans to give
you hope and a future."

(Jeremiah 29:11)

God has all days planned for us. We may not always listen to His voice and what He says to us, but He still loves us and gives us so much hope for the future. He will never harm us, and He keeps us protected. Bad things do happen, but God still is with us. God doesn't force us to make certain choices, but gives us free will.

What are some things you have done that have been God's calling on your life?

Write a list of times when you felt God wasn't with you, but later knew He was, and it was His timing, not yours.

Prayer:

God, take my hand and lead me in the direction You want me to go. I don't want to take my life and our relationship for granted. I want to walk with You in all I do and in all areas of my life. Thank You for helping me along the way.

Day 3

Praise be to the God and Father of our Lord Jesus Christ! In His great mercy, He has given us new birth into a living hope through the resurrection of Jesus Christ from the dead, and into an inheritance that can never perish, spoil, or fade. This inheritance is kept in heaven for you, who through faith are shielded by God's power until the coming of the salvation that is ready to be revealed in the last time.

(1 Peter 1:3–5)

We have such great hope through the power of Jesus's resurrection from the dead. We can know that He is alive to give us great hope and new birth. We can know that we will spend eternity in heaven, and that it lasts forever. More than ever, now is the time to come to Jesus and give yourself to Him. Do you wonder what peace and hope feels like? How about the joy it gives you to know that you have that unconditional love holding you and protecting you. You need not wait any longer. Take that gift today and keep moving forward.

What can you praise God for today? Have you given your life to Jesus?

If Jesus were to ask you today to be His friend and walk alongside Him, how would that make you feel? Now, seeing that question, did you know He does ask you to walk alongside Him so you may have that eternal reward someday.

Prayer:

Jesus, I want to thank You for hope. I ask You to come into my life today and help me to live each day to the best I can so others can see You in me and my walk. I want that living hope so I can have eternal life with You. Thank You for all You have done for me. I want to be a living testimony for You.

Day 4

Therefore, since we have been justified through faith, we have peace with God through our Lord Jesus Christ, through whom we have gained access by faith into this grace in which we now stand. And we boast in the hope of the glory of God. Not only so, but we also glory in our sufferings because we know that suffering produces perseverance, character, and hope. And hope does not put us to shame because God's love has been poured into our hearts through the Holy Spirit, who has been given to us.

(Romans 5:1–5)

While we don't understand why we have to go through suffering, God has given us perseverance, character, and hope. The things we go through may not be what we have in mind with life, but God's love has been poured into our hearts.

Even if we don't understand at the time, it is our faith that gets us through and dictates how we react to the sufferings in life. Some things never get easier, but with God you will have the hope for what He is showing you to make it through.

What are some of your trials and sufferings when you knew you had to trust God to make it through?

What can you do to let God know you have trust in and hope through Him?

Prayer:

God, when life gets me down, I want to trust You. I am sorry for not always feeling the hope You have given me. Help me to understand that You are the hope in all circumstances, no matter what life throws at me. I will do my best to trust You.

Day 5

For in this hope we were saved.
But hope that is seen is no hope at all.
Who hopes for what they already have?
But if we hope for what we do not yet
have, we wait for it patiently.

(Romans 8:24–25)

Are you patient with what you have prayed for but not yet received? Do you have the hope of knowing that your prayers will be answered one day the way God sees best for you? Or are you wanting everything answered your way? God has His timing and His way. Life isn't about get, get, get! It is about thanking Him for what He has and hasn't done for us.

Do you believe you are saved? Is there something holding you back?

In times of need or sorrow, we don't feel God has given us anything, but He has given us so much. What has He given you?

Prayer:

I trust Your word to give me hope, to build me up. I patiently wait for what You have in store for me. I pray for the hope to help me while reaching for Your hand to carry me through. Thank You for being patient with me and helping me through.

Day 6

Be joyful in hope, patient in affliction, faithful in prayer.

(Romans 12:12)

This explains itself in more than one way. Spending time in prayer brings you closer to God and will definitely help you feel the hope that will give you joy. It also helps you be patient while waiting for the answers to prayer. Don't trust the process of what you are going through. Trust only in what God has for you. Suffering can be hard to understand, but be trust in God, knowing His ways are best for us in all that happens.

What type of suffering have you gone through knowing that God would come through in His timing?

Write a list of prayers for others so you can remind yourself to keep praying.

Prayer:

Lord, thank You for the life You have given me and the patience to keep myself going in all circumstances. Help me to be thankful and trust that You are in control.

Day 7

Now faith is confidence in what we hope for
and assurance about what we do not see.

(Hebrews 11:1)

We sometimes feel that we need to see things to believe. It's like the wind—we can feel it, we know it is there, but we can't see it. Or maybe air as we breathe. We can feel God's presence without seeing Him. You can feel Him in your heart and in your mind. His presence is so powerful, but we don't always acknowledge He is there because we have so much going on in our life.

Take a few moments and soak into God's presence. What are you feeling at this moment?

What is something you can do to know and feel God? How do you personally know God is with you?

Prayer:

Lord, help me to feel You and Your presence. Help me to understand that I won't always feel You, but I can still know You are there with me. Thank You for always being with me in good times and the times I don't feel things are going so well.

Day 8

Love is patient; love is kind. It does not envy; it does not boast; it is not proud. It does not dishonor others; it is not self-seeking; it is not easily angered; it keeps no record of wrongs. Love does not delight in evil, but rejoices with the truth. It always protects, always trusts, always hopes, always perseveres.

(1 Corinthians 13: 4–7)

And now these three remain: faith, hope, and love. But the greatest of these is love.

(1 Corinthians 13:13)

God is love, so while looking into these verses, put God's name in the place of the word love. Love is a strong word, but so easily misused in our world today. Some may use it in simple terms, not really meaning love in the sense that it should be used. Faith and hope will help us get through the tough times, but God (love) is the only answer to walk with us and take us on the journey that lies ahead.

Are you ready to step into faith and know that we can have hope with God?

Take it a step further, and read the 1 Corinthians 13. Take notes on what it means to you.

Where does your faith, love, and hope come from? Is it money, food, other people? Take a moment and reflect on your life. Do you put God first or other things or people?

Prayer:

Lord, thank You for keeping me in check with what You want in my life. I understand that I do not always put my hope in You. But, God, I want that in my life. I want my hope to be in You.

Day 9

*We have this hope as an anchor for the soul,
firm and secure. It enters the inner sanctuary
behind the curtain, where our forerunner,
Jesus, has entered on our behalf...*

(Hebrews 6:19–20)

An anchor holds down the ship. God holds us grounded with His word. Let's take a moment and just think about what His word says. John 8:32 says, "and you shall know the truth, and the truth shall set you free." This verse can hold you grounded to His word, knowing what the truth is. You can understand and embrace what He has given us in the Bible to live on. Taking this and knowing what to stand on, no matter what comes your way or what you have been through.

What has happened in your life that keeps you from feeling set free?

Do you have something heavy on or wrong in your heart today?

Prayer:

Lord, help me to let go of this heavy anchor and understand that You are the anchor to my soul. I can rely on You and give it to You to carry for me.

Day 10

Paul, a servant of God and an apostle of Jesus Christ to further the faith of God's elect and their knowledge of the truth that leads to godliness—in the hope of eternal life, which God, who does not lie, promised before the beginning of time, and which now at his appointed season he has brought to light through the preaching entrusted to me by the command of God our Savior.

(Titus 1:1–3)

God's promise to us is eternal life. This Scripture shows us that when we have hope, faith, knowledge, and trust, we will live a godly life. Knowing that you have faith in God's promise.

Do you trust in God at all times or only when it is convenient for you? Do you spend time with Him in good times and bad? Or only when you are desperate for answers.

Take a moment, thank Him, and believe He is with you right now. What are some things you can thank Him for?

Prayer:

Lord, I want to trust You and believe in all times that You are with me. Each day, I want to come to You and ask for Your knowledge on how to live the life You desire for me. Thank You for allowing me to not always be strong. I know I can always come back to You, and You will be there with open arms.

Day 11

While we wait for the blessed hope — the appearing of the glory of our great God and Savior, Jesus Christ, who gave Himself for us to redeem us from all wickedness and to purify for Himself a people that are His very own, eager to do what is good.

These, then, are the things you should teach. Encourage and rebuke with all authority. Do not let anyone despise you.

(Titus 2:13–15)

What powerful words are you living and teaching others in the truth? Or are you just going about your day? We should be an example as we live our life. Some may talk the talk, but not walk the walk. None of us is perfect, but we should show our actions to others as what a Christ follower lives like. Have you asked Jesus in your heart? If you have wronged someone, go and ask for forgiveness, not just from them but for you to feel the love in your heart.

Think of those whom you have wronged. Have you asked for forgiveness?

How are you living your life? Are you showing others you are a Christ follower? Whom can you reach out to today to share the Gospels with?

Prayer:

Lord, please help me to live the life that pleases You. I want to be an example for those around me and those who listen to my words and watch my actions.

Day 12

See what great love the Father has lavished on us, that we should be called children of God! And that is what we are! The reason the world does not know us is that it did not know Him. Dear friends, now we are children of God, and what we will be has not yet been made known. But we know that when Christ appears, we shall be like Him, for we shall see Him as He is. All who have this hope in Him purify themselves, just as He is pure.

(1 John 3:1–3)

Oh, what a glorious day that will be when my Jesus I shall see. We are His children, and He loves us unconditionally. We will be with Him one day. Many have left before us, but we know we shall see them again, as we are His children. As Father, He wants what is best for us. He wants us to live the best we can so others will see Him in us, and they will come to know and follow Him. Life will never be perfect, but Jesus is. He will forever be there for us. Become more like Jesus.

Take a moment to listen to the song "What a Day That Will Be." Feel in the moment how much God loves you and wants what is best for you.

As a child of God, what are some characteristics He has given you that you can thank Him for? Whom can you share Jesus with today?

Prayer:

Lord, I am honored to be Your child. I want to live the life You want for me. Please show me what I can do for You as Your child.

Day 13

When Herod saw Jesus, he was greatly pleased
because for a long time, he had been wanting
to see Him. From what he had heard about
Him, he hoped to see Him perform a sign
of some sort. He plied Him with many
questions, but Jesus gave him no answer.

(Luke 23:8–9)

We may expect Jesus to perform a miracle right now, but He answers in His time, and it may not be the answer you are looking for. He doesn't make bad things happen, and He is with you at all times. We may cry out to Him, especially when we are desperate for an answer or for a sign, but it doesn't mean He is going to answer right now. He doesn't love us any less. It's okay to ask Him questions; you will soon get an answer. Just be patient.

Do you have some unanswered prayers? Write a list.

Are there prayers that were answered, but not with what you requested? Do you know that the answers you received are what is best for you? Write a list.

Prayer:

Lord, I want to thank You for the answers You have given me and for the ones I haven't received yet, but I know they are in Your timing and Your way. Thank You for giving me the life I have and for the love You have for me.

Day 14

Who is going to harm you if you are eager to do good? But even if you should suffer for what is right, you are blessed. "Do not fear their threat; do not be frightened." But in your hearts revere Christ as Lord. Always be prepared to give an answer to everyone who asks you to give the reason for the hope that you have. But do this with gentleness and respect, keeping a clear conscience, so that those who speak maliciously against your good behavior in Christ may be ashamed of their slander.

(1 Peter 3:13–16)

You may be asked why you believe the way you do. Keep in mind that people may not understand the love you have. You have peace and hope, love and joy. Do you know how to answer the ones who are questioning you? Will you answer with a gentle spirit or get defensive? God wants you to answer with a gentle voice with the love that comes from Him. It may be easy to argue and fight back, but keep calm and have an open heart. There is way too much arguing and fighting in this world over things that are unnecessary.

Keep your faith!

Make a list of people whom you can talk to about your beliefs. Keep in mind the ones who have questioned you.

Pray for the right words to say and keep a calm spirit while communicating what God wants for you to share.

Prayer:

Lord, thank You for the words that I can speak to others. Thank You for the calm spirit and gentle voice to reach the hurting and unsaved.

Day 15

And this water symbolizes baptism that now saves you also—not the removal of dirt from the body, but the pledge of a clear conscience toward God. It saves you by the resurrection of Jesus Christ, who has gone into heaven and is at God's right hand—with angels, authorities, and powers in submission to Him.

(1 Peter 3:21–22)

Giving your whole self to Jesus is really important for your salvation. But professing publicly your love for Jesus by Baptism shows you are in Him, and you want to share with all that you are in Him. You are making a public pledge.

Have you made that decision to publicly share your faith? If not, why have you chosen not to? If you have, what helped you make that decision, and how did it change your life?

Prayer:

Lord, help me to understand more the meaning of water baptism, and show me what I can do or say to help others with the decision.

Day 16

*But in your hearts revere Christ as Lord.
Always be prepared to give an answer to everyone
who asks you to give the reason for the hope
that you have. But do this with gentleness
and respect, keeping a clear conscience, so
that those who speak maliciously against your
good behavior in Christ may be ashamed
of their slander. For it is better, if it is God's
will, to suffer for doing good than for doing evil.*

(1 Peter 3:15–17)

What powerful verses. Being prepared to live as Christ is good behavior. You may be slandered. How will you react? You are to give answers with a gentle heart. Not with anger or malice. Living life for Jesus is what is going to help you share with others, not show fear or lose hope. But gain hope with what God has offered you. Life can seem so draining at times, but taking the love, peace, and hope and allowing others to see it in you can make a difference.

I would recommend you read 1 Peter 3.

What are these words telling you? Look inside your heart and see if there is anything you can do differently while sharing the love of Christ and what He has done for you.

Prayer:

Lord, I ask You to take away any anger or bitterness I have and help me have gentle answers when sharing Your word and living my life to the fullest. Help me have peace within me.

Day 17

But Christ is faithful as the Son
over God's house. And we are His house,
if indeed we hold firmly to our confidence
and the hope in which we glory.

(Hebrews 3:6)

We are a part of the household of God. We are the temple, the church, when we hold on to His confidence. Are you sincere in His glory? Think about the hope we have in Him. It's not just for the things in life that are going well, but for what takes us under in the realm of life.

Read Hebrews 3:7–19.

What are these words telling you? Have you got a hardened heart? Do you believe that Christ is faithful? Why or why not?

Prayer:

Thank You for the confidence You have given me. Lord, You are my guide, my stronghold, and I will be forever grateful that You have taken care of me and those around me. Thank You for all You have done and all You are about to do. I want to be Your church.

Day 18

*Even though we speak like this, dear friends,
we are convinced of better things in your
case—the things that have to do with
salvation. God is not unjust; He will not
forget your work and the love you have
shown Him as you have helped His people
and continue to help them. We want each of
you to show this same diligence to the very
end so that what you hope for may be
fully realized. We do not want you to
become lazy, but to imitate those who
through faith and patience inherit what
has been promised.*

(Hebrews 6: 9–12)

God doesn't forget your work. He keeps us going and sees all we do for Him. He doesn't want us to become lazy; He will keep us motivated and strong. Doing His work isn't always the easiest, but with a willing heart, you will make it through, and the rewards will be worth it. You will inherit what has been promised to you.

Have you gotten lazy with doing His work? What can you do differently to make sure you are showing diligence?

What work can you do for Him now? Do you feel you need the rewards to be bold? Where can you see them right now, or is it something you trust God with?

Prayer:

Lord, Your word says to keep diligent until the end. Help me do what You are asking of me and show me what You want me to do? I want to be faithful and motivated in doing Your work. My heart and arms are open.

Day 19

The former regulation is set aside because it was weak and useless (for the law made nothing perfect), and a better hope is introduced, by which we draw near to God.

(Hebrews 7: 18–19)

The new way to live is through Jesus. Jesus paid the price for all of us, not just some. Those who draw near will have a better life knowing that He has given you something beautiful. You have hope in knowing Him and knowing that He is your protector and will guide you through everything. The good and the bad. He will never leave you, nor forsake you.

Have you opened your heart to receive the hope you deserve? Today is the day to do just that. Pray the prayer and give it all to Him.

Prayer:

Lord, please come into my heart and give me the hope I desire. I want to receive You today. Open my heart to what You have for me, not just in the bad times, but in the times I can rejoice in what You have given me. Thank You for the love You have shown me.

Day 20

Remember that at that time you were separate from Christ, excluded from citizenship in Israel and foreigners to the covenants of the promise, without hope and without God in the world. But now in Christ Jesus you who once were far away have been brought near by the blood of Christ.

(Ephesians 2:12–13)

As you get to know Jesus more, you will not want to turn back to your old ways. He will be with you always. Hebrews 13:5 and Deuteronomy 31:6 say that He will never leave you or forsake you. You will still have fear, but you can also trust in what He will do for you. Your life won't be perfect, but knowing God is with you always is such a comfort.

Read Hebrews 13:5 and Deuteronomy 31:6. What do these mean to you? I encourage you to find more Scriptures that talk about being with you always.

Day 21

For this reason, ever since I heard about your faith in the Lord Jesus and your love for all God's people, I have not stopped giving thanks for you, remembering you in my prayers. I keep asking that the God of our Lord Jesus Christ, the glorious Father, may give you the Spirit of wisdom and revelation, so that you may know Him better. I pray that the eyes of your heart may be enlightened in order that you may know the hope to which He has called you, the riches of His glorious inheritance in His holy people, and His incomparably great power for us who believe. That power is the same as the mighty strength He exerted when He raised Christ from the dead and seated Him at His right hand in the heavenly realms, far above all rule and authority, power and dominion, and every name that is invoked, not only in the present age but also in the one to come. And God placed all things under His feet and appointed Him to be head over everything for the church, which is His body, the fullness of Him who fills everything in every way.

(Ephesians 1: 15–23)

Those who have the love of the Lord will find the good in others, giving thanks in circumstances that are beyond their control. Living life to the fullest and for the Lord will and can change your outlook on life and others. Pray for others to come to know Jesus, even those who have hurt you. Keep in mind that we are all God's children. We are not to turn our back on their salvation. Give each and every person and situation to God.

Who has hurt you? Pray for them today. Pray for their salvation and give the situation to God.

Are you holding on to anger or bitterness towards anyone? Ask God to help you let them go so you give the situation and person to God. I would encourage you to read Ephesians 1.

Prayer:

Lord, I want to thank You for giving me words to say to the ones who have hurt me so that they may open their hearts to You, that they may come to You for guidance and give it all to You. Also, help me overcome the hurt that has been caused me. Guide my heart and words not to harm others.

Day 22

See what great love the Father has lavished on us, that we should be called children of God! And that is what we are! The reason the world does not know us is that it did not know Him. Dear friends, now we are children of God, and what we will be has not yet been made known. But we know that when Christ appears, we shall be like Him, for we shall see Him as He is. All who have this hope in Him purify themselves, just as He is pure.

(1 John 3:1-3)

Some of you may have not had an earthly father, or he has gone to be with the Lord. Scriptures clearly state that God is our Father. Confiding in Him and knowing He has our hearts in His hands, you can trust that He will do what is best for you. That is what a good father does. He is a good father who will not harm you, but keep you in His hands. He holds your future and all you do.

Have you looked at God as your Father? If not, tell Him today that He is your Heavenly Father, and you want a relationship with Him. Take a moment and make a list of the things you can tell Him. Put on that list how you feel about Him being your Father and everything else you have held in and not shared with anyone else.

Prayer:

Lord, Father God, I want to thank You today for being my dad. Thank You for taking care of me and giving me guidance in my life. I trust You and give my whole self to You.

Day 23

Send me your light and your
faithful care, let them lead me;
let them bring me to your holy
mountain, to the place where you dwell.
Then I will go to the altar of God,
to God, my joy and my delight.
I will praise You with the lyre,
O God, my God.

Why, my soul, are you downcast?
Why so disturbed within me?
Put your hope in God,
for I will yet praise Him,
my Savior and my God.

(Psalm 43:3–5)

You can find delight in the Lord. You will have down days, but finding joy in the Lord will give you hope. Praise and lift up His name so you can feel His delight and know that He is forever with you. When you are having a conversation with someone, stay uplifted and joyful. Don't let others get you down. Keep connected and praise His name. Love the Lord with all your heart and mind each day. Keep rejoicing!

What are some ways you can praise His name today? Will you share the love you have even if you are having a bad day?

Can you think of someone with whom you can share His message?

Prayer:

Lord, I want to praise You at all times, not just when I am having a good day. Help me to see what I need to change, and help me to see how to change my way of thinking and speaking.

Day 24

Eat honey, my son, for it is good;
honey from the comb is sweet to your taste.
Know also that wisdom is like honey for you:
If you find it, there is a future hope for you,
and your hope will not be cut off.

(Proverbs 24:13–14)

Wisdom from God's word is a sweet taste in your mouth. His word gives us hope, and we know that it will get us where we need to be. Reading His word and applying it to our life is a stronghold; it helps us to keep moving forward, no matter what life throws at us. Don't allow others to get you down; just keep moving forward.

When you think of God's word, what does the sweetness taste like?

What does your future hope look like? Where does your hope come from?

Prayer:

Lord, please help me to move in the direction You want me to, so I can know for certain I have hope in You and my future. I want the strength to move so close to You that every move I make is in You.

Day 25

*Brothers and sisters, we do not want you to be uninformed
about those who sleep in death, so that you do not grieve like
the rest of mankind, who have no hope. For we believe that Jesus
died and rose again, and so we believe that God will bring with
Jesus those who have fallen asleep in Him. According to the
Lord's word, we tell you that we who are still alive, who are left
until the coming of the Lord, will certainly not precede those
who have fallen asleep. For the Lord Himself will come down
from heaven, with a loud command, with the voice of the arch-
angel and with the trumpet call of God, and the dead in Christ
will rise first. After that, we who are still alive and are left will
be caught up together with them in the clouds to meet the Lord
in the air. And so we will be with the Lord forever.
Therefore, encourage one another with these words.*

(1 Thessalonians 4:13–18)

All those who have believed and have passed on before us will be with Jesus when He returns. What a beautiful feeling to know that even if we are with the Lord in heaven, we will still be with Him after His return. Imagine the feeling of being in the presence of the Lord. We can rejoice knowing we won't have any more heartache or pain. All our sickness will be gone for good.

When you get to see Jesus face-to-face, what will you want to say to Him? Can you find it in your heart to speak to Him now and communicate what you are feeling?

Prayer:

Lord, You are my life, and I am so thankful that I know I will see You again soon. My life is in You, and I consider it an honor to know that I will be with You forever one day. Thank You for answering prayers and showing me what is best for me.

Day 26

Command those who are rich in this present world not to be arrogant nor to put their hope in wealth, which is so uncertain, but to put their hope in God, who richly provides us with everything for our enjoyment. Command them to do good, to be rich in good deeds, and to be generous and willing to share. In this way they will lay up treasure for themselves as a firm foundation for the coming age, so that they may take hold of the life that is truly life.

(1 Timothy 6:17–19)

Some people want to put their hope in wealth, and that should not be so. Our hope should be in God. He will provide for you. That doesn't mean we don't have to work and take care of our bills, but trust when there is a need. Don't do your good deeds for yourself, but for the good of others. Being rich in deeds will allow you to feel better about life.

What are some good deeds you can do to help someone else? For whom can you do the deeds?

Prayer:

Lord, please help me to do what I need to do to help others so I am not just thinking about myself. Allow me to share my faith and love for You as part of my deeds. I want my life to be consistent for You, Lord.

Day 27

*If you continue in your faith, established
and firm, and do not move from the hope
held out in the Gospel. This is the Gospel
that you heard and that has been proclaimed
to every creature under heaven, and of which
I, Paul, have become a servant.*

(Colossians 1:23)

Do you still have your faith? Continue your faith and stay firm at all times. Don't waver as some are used to doing. Proclaim His love to every one and in all circumstances. He will lift you up in His arms, as He knows what you are going through. Keep the spark going and don't let it burn out. What can you do to keep your flame going and to stay firm in your beliefs?

Read Colossians 1: 24–29.

Prayer:

Lord, thank You for helping me to keep my beliefs in You. I want to continue to stay strong and firm in what You have taught me. My life is in You, and I want to continue living for You.

Day 28

*Therefore, since we have been justified
through faith, we have peace with God
through our Lord Jesus Christ, through
whom we have gained access by faith into
this grace in which we now stand. And we
boast in the hope of the glory of God. Not
only so, but we also glory in our sufferings
because we know that suffering produces
perseverance, character, and hope. And hope
does not put us to shame because God's love
has been poured out into our hearts through
the Holy Spirit, who has been given to us.*

(Romans 5:1–5)

What powerful words. It is hard to suffer, but harder to see someone you love suffer. Take note that you will persevere, and your character will stay strong. Hope in the Lord doesn't put us to shame, and it can keep us going. We can have the peace of all understanding that comes with it. Life isn't always easy; it is how we react to and look at it that matters. Stay strong and remember the hope that comes from the Lord.

Read James 1:12. What is this verse saying to you?

Are you going through trials? What are they?

Prayer:

Lord, You are my strength and hope. Thank You for the peace I can have while going through trials, and thank You for the peace I can have seeing others go through trials. I ask You for help through the times I don't feel the peace.

Day 29

Hope deferred makes the heart sick,
but a longing fulfilled is a tree of life.

Whoever scorns instruction will pay for it,
but whoever respects a command is rewarded.

The teaching of the wise is a fountain of life,
turning a person from the snares of death.

Good judgment wins favor,
but the way of the unfaithful
leads to their destruction.

(Proverbs 13:12–15)

Where is your heart today? Is it deferred or are you taking the road to respecting the commands of life? It clearly states that good judgment wins favor. Teach others to have favor in the Lord and trust that He gives us hope. Be wise in your teaching and stay faithful.

Is your heart wise today? If not, what can you do to change that?

What are you teaching those around you?

Prayer:

Lord, I want to lead others to You, not away. Help me make good judgments and choices to be an example and have words to say. Help me say the right words and not go astray.

Day 30

You are my refuge and my shield;
I have put my hope in Your word.

(Psalms 119:114)

God's word is so powerful. We are not to take it lightly, as some are used to doing. We understand that He is always with us. No matter what is going on in our life. He will protect us from evil and give us the strength to shield us from what can harm us. Are things going to be perfect? Absolutely not, but knowing He is with us through the good and the bad will carry us through. Stay strong, not just for yourself but for those around you whom you love.

What barrier are you putting in front of the shield?

What have you put in front of the hope you can have in Him?

Prayer:

Lord, I have put my hope in You! You are my shield and protector, and I want to thank You for that.

Day 31

I sought the Lord, and He answered me;
He delivered me from all my fears.
Those who look to Him are radiant;
their faces are never covered with shame.
This poor man called, and the Lord heard him;
He saved him out of all his troubles.

(Psalms 34:4–6)

We don't have to fear what has happened or what is going to happen. Seek the Lord, and He will save you from all your troubles. Again, your life won't be perfect, but God is perfect for you. He delivers us with hope from the pain others have caused us. He wants you to smile and not feel ashamed.

Is something in your life causing you to feel shamed? Something you did? Who has hurt you, and whom have you hurt? What are the hurts?

Prayer:

Lord, thank You for taking away my shame and pain. I feel radiant in You and the love You have covered me with. Thank You for taking away my troubles and helping me through my trials and hurts. I will live my life for You so I can show others what You have done for me.

Optional

For God so loved the world that He gave His one and only Son, that whoever believes in Him shall not perish but have eternal life.

(John 3:16)

God sent His Son to give us eternal life. Are you ready to give it all to Him and trust in the hope He has for you? Today is the day, no matter what you have chosen in your life. He is always there with you. He will forgive you, but you have to make that choice to give it all to Him.

Prayer:

Lord, I give my life to You today. I don't want to hurt You, but I know I will over and over. I ask for Your forgiveness for what I have done. Help me to understand what You have given me and the hope I can have in You today. Thank You for all You have done for me.

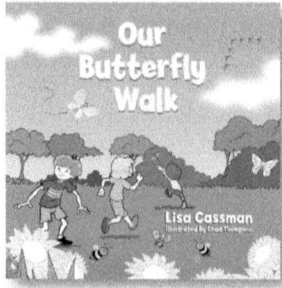

Our Butterfly Walk
ISBN Hardcover: 978-1-63765-724-9
ISBN Paperback: 978-1-63765-723-2

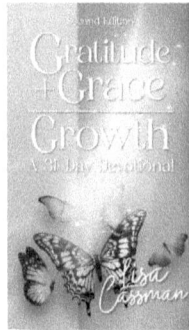

Gratitude + Grace = Growth: A 31-Day Devotional
ISBN Paperback: 978-1-63765-609-9

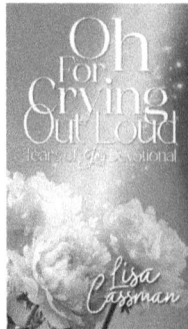

Oh For Crying Out Loud: Tears of Joy Devotional
ISBN Paperback: 978-1-63765-586-3

Finding the Beautiful You
ISBN Paperback: 978-1-61244-601-1

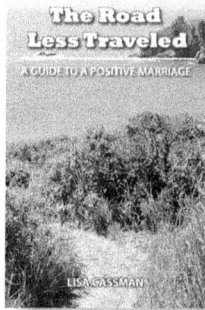

The Road Less Traveled
ISBN Paperback: 978-1-61244-502-1

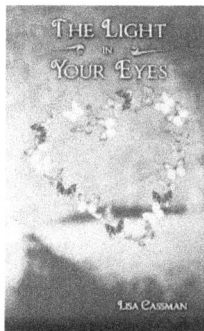

The Light in Your Eyes
ISBN Paperback: 978-1-61244-304-1

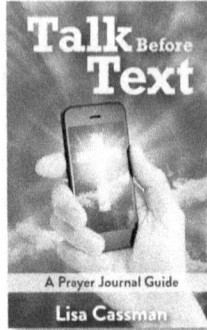

Talk Before Text: A Prayer Journal Guide
ISBN Paperback: 978-1-61244-777-3

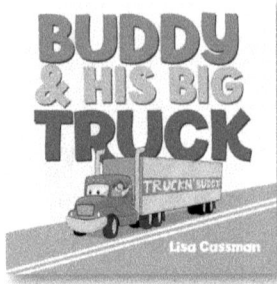

Buddy and His Big Truck
ISBN Hardcover: 978-1-63765-001-1
ISBN Paperback: 978-1-61244-991-3

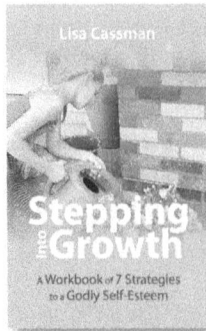

Stepping Into Growth:
A Workbook of 7 Strategies to a Godly Self-Esteem
ISBN Paperback: 978-1-63765-185-8

www.ingramcontent.com/pod-product-compliance
Lightning Source LLC
Chambersburg PA
CBHW052009090426
42741CB00008B/1621